SPIRITUALS
FOR UKULELE

ISBN 978-1-5400-1245-6

Copyright © 2018 by HAL LEONARD LLC
International Copyright Secured   All Rights Reserved

7777 W. BLUEMOUND RD. P.O. BOX 13819 MILWAUKEE, WI 53213

In Australia Contact:
Hal Leonard Australia Pty. Ltd.
4 Lentara Court
Cheltenham, Victoria, 3192 Australia
Email: ausadmin@halleonard.com.au

All My Trials

African-American Spiritual

be o - ver. _____ Too late, my

broth - ers, _____ too late, but nev - er mind. _____

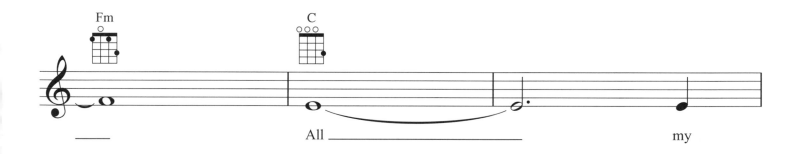

_____ All _____ my

tri - als, Lord, _____ will soon _____

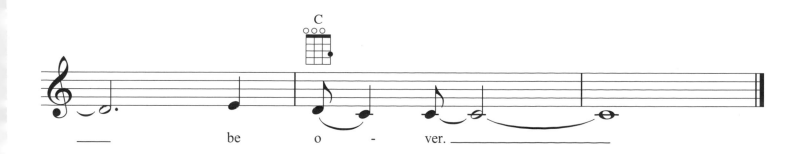

_____ be o - ver. _____

Deep River

African-American Spiritual
Based on Joshua 3

Every Time I Feel the Spirit

African-American Spritual

Ev - 'ry time I ___ feel the Spir - it ___ mov - ing in my heart, __ I will

pray. ___ Yes, ev - 'ry time I ___ feel the Spir - it ___ mov - ing

in my heart, __ I will pray. 1. Up - on the moun - tain, ___ my Lord
2. Jor - dan Riv - er ___ runs right

spoke. Out His mouth came __ fire and smoke. All a - round me ___ looks so
cold. Chills the bod - y, ___ not the soul. Ain't but one train __ on this

shine. Ask my Lord if ___ all was mine. Ev - 'ry
track. Runs to heav - en ___ and right back. Ev - 'ry

pray.

Do Lord

Traditional

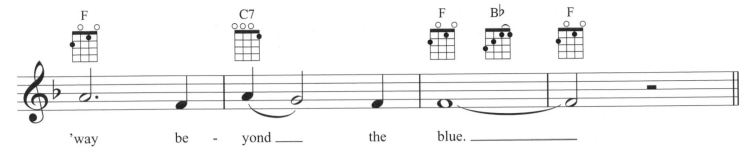

'way be - yond _____ the blue. _____

Chorus

Do Lord, oh, do Lord, oh, do re - mem - ber

me. Do Lord, oh, do Lord, oh, do re - mem - ber

me. Do Lord, oh, do Lord, oh, do re - mem - ber

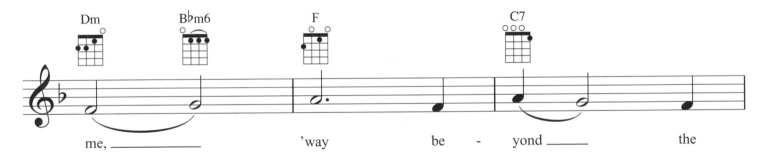

me, _____ 'way be - yond _____ the

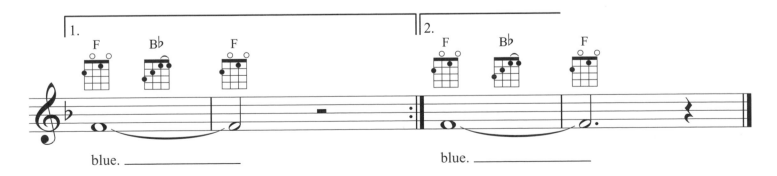

blue. _____   blue. _____

Down by the Riverside

African-American Spiritual

Give Me Jesus

African-American Spiritual

Go Down, Moses

Traditional American Spiritual

He's Got the Whole World in His Hands

Traditional Spiritual

in His hands. ___ He's got the wind and the rain ___

in His hands. ___ He's got the whole world in His

Verse

hands. 3. He's got ev - 'ry - bod - y here ___ in His hands. ___ He's got

ev - 'ry - bod - y here ___ in His hands. ___ He's got ev - 'ry - bod - y here ___

in His hands. ___ He's got the whole world in His hands.

I'm Gonna Sing
When the Spirit Says Sing

African-American Spiritual

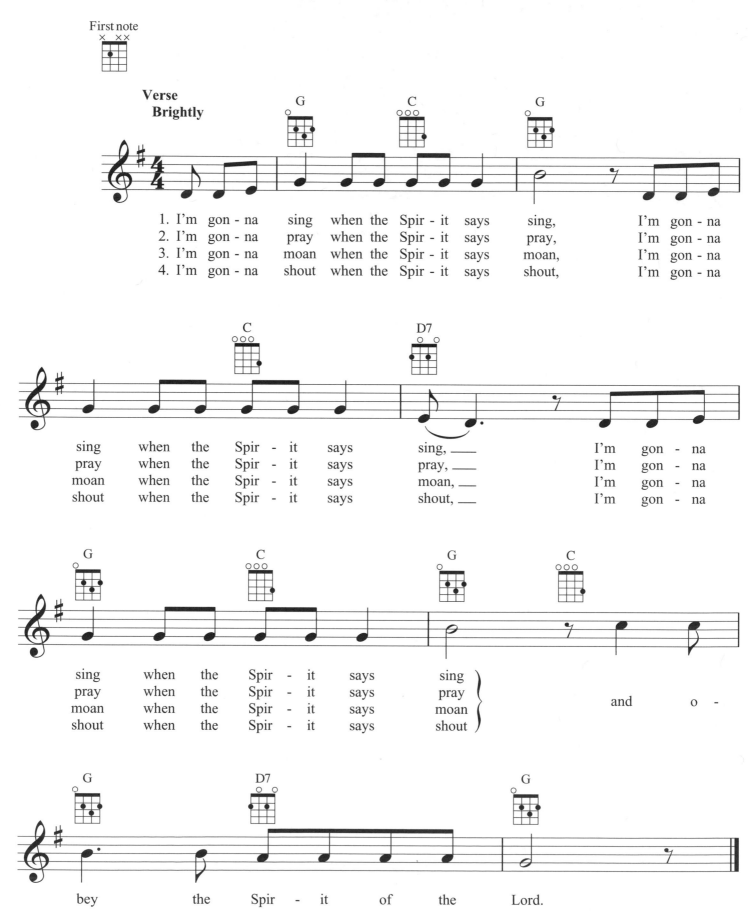

Jacob's Ladder

African-American Spiritual

Joshua
(Fit the Battle of Jericho)
African-American Spiritual

Additional Lyrics

2. 'Way up to the walls of Jericho
He marched with a spear in hand.
"Go blow the ram's horn," Joshua cried,
"'Cause the battle is in my hands."

3. Then the lamb, ram, sheep horns began to blow
And the trumpets began to sound;
And Joshua commanded the children to shout
And the walls came tumblin' down.

Kum Ba Yah

Traditional Spiritual

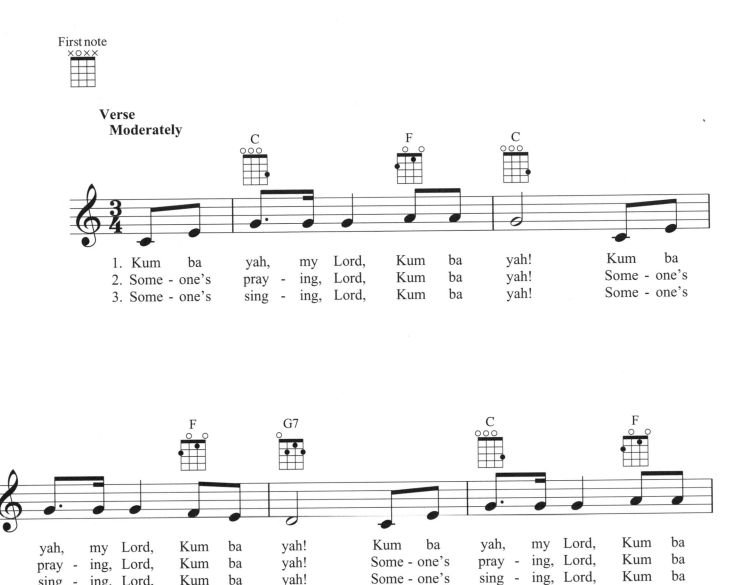

Let Us Break Bread Together

Traditional Spiritual

The Lonesome Road

African-American Spiritual

Additional Lyrics

2. Look down, look down that lonesome road,
Hang down your head and cry.
I loved, I lost, my days are numbered.
O Lord, I want to die.

3. Look down, look down that lonesome road,
Where love has come and gone.
Look up, look up, you'll find a new love.
Look up and keep trav'lin' on.

My Lord, What a Morning

African-American Spiritual

Never Said a Mumblin' Word

(He Never Said a Mumblin' Word)

African-American Spiritual

Nobody Knows the Trouble I've Seen

African-American Spiritual

First note

Chorus
Soulfully

No - bod - y knows the trou - ble I've seen,

no - bod - y knows but Je - sus. No - bod - y knows the

To Coda

trou - ble I've seen, glo - ry hal - le -

Verse

lu - jah! 1. Some - times I'm up, some - times I'm down,

2.–5. See additional lyrics

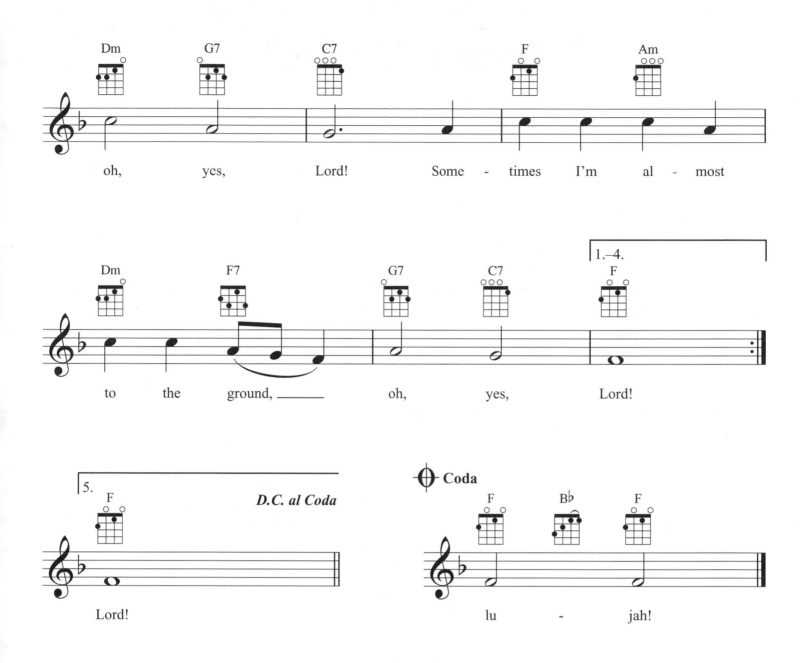

oh,　　　　yes,　　　　Lord!　　　　Some - times　I'm　al - most

to　　　the　　　ground, _____　oh,　　yes,　　Lord!

5.

D.C. al Coda

Lord!

Coda

lu - jah!

Additional Lyrics

2. Now, you may think that I don't know,
   Oh, yes, Lord;
   But I've had my troubles here below,
   Oh, yes, Lord.

3. One day while I was walkin' along,
   Oh, yes, Lord;
   The sky opened up and love came down,
   Oh, yes, Lord.

4. What made ol' Satan hate me so?
   Oh, yes, Lord;
   He had me once and had to let me go,
   Oh, yes, Lord.

5. I never shall forget that day,
   Oh, yes, Lord;
   When Jesus washed my sins away,
   Oh, yes, Lord.

Rock-A-My Soul

African-American Spiritual

First note

Oh,   rock - a - my   soul ___ in   the   bos - om   of   A - bra - ham,

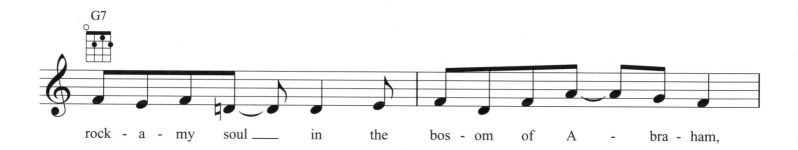

rock - a - my   soul ___ in   the   bos - om   of   A - bra - ham,

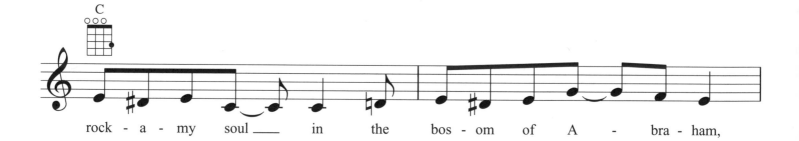

rock - a - my   soul ___ in   the   bos - om   of   A - bra - ham,

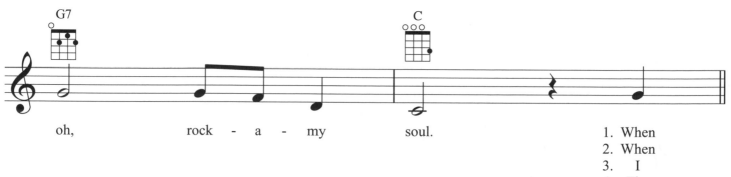

oh,   rock - a - my   soul.

1. When
2. When
3. I
4. The

Verse

I went down to the val - ley to pray,
I came home from the val - ley at night,
felt so sad on the morn - ing be - fore,
sun shines bright on the cloud - i - est day,

oh, rock - a - my soul. My
oh, rock - a - my soul. I
oh, rock - a - my soul. I
oh, rock - a - my soul. A

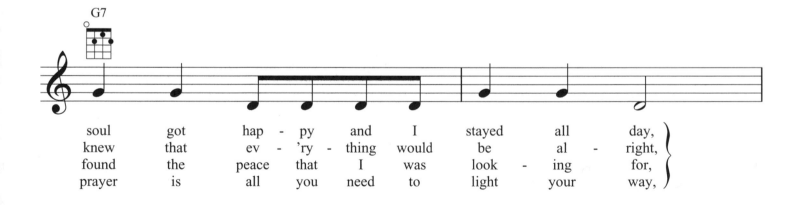

soul got hap - py and I stayed all day,
knew that ev - 'ry - thing would be al - right,
found the peace that I was look - ing for,
prayer is all you need to light your way,

1.–3.

4.

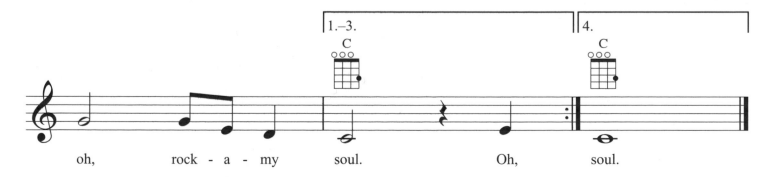

oh, rock - a - my soul. Oh, soul.

25

Somebody's Knockin' at Your Door

African-American Spiritual

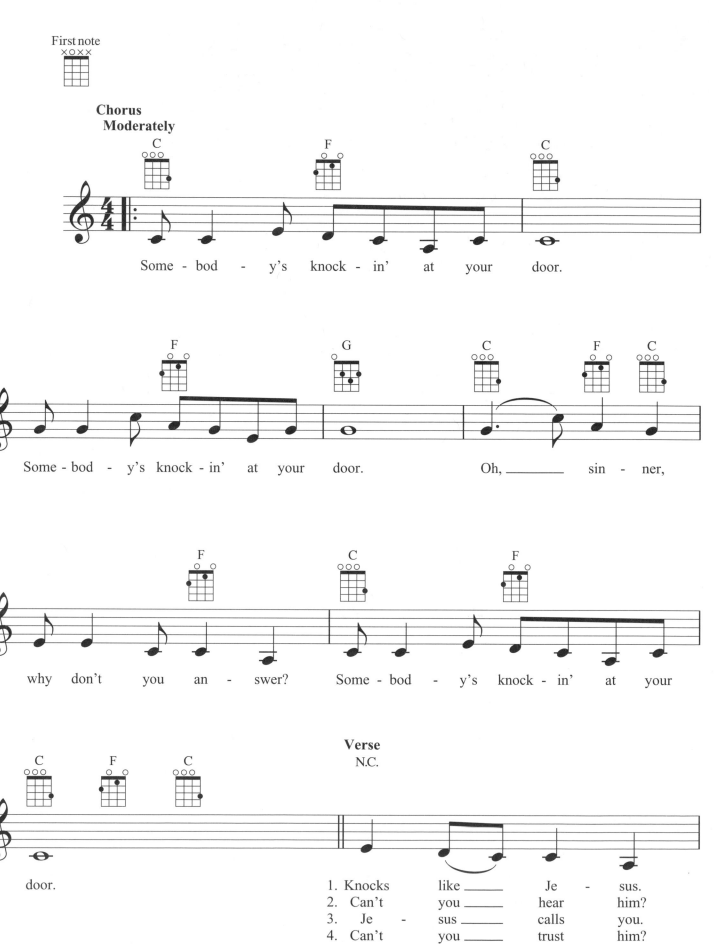

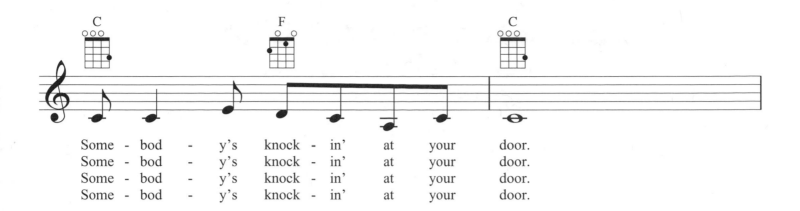

Some - bod - y's knock - in' at your door.
Some - bod - y's knock - in' at your door.
Some - bod - y's knock - in' at your door.
Some - bod - y's knock - in' at your door.

Knocks like ____ Je - sus.
Can't you ____ hear him?
Je - sus ____ calls you.
Can't you ____ trust him?

Some - bod - y's knock - in' at your

door. Oh, _____ sin - ner, why don't you an - swer?

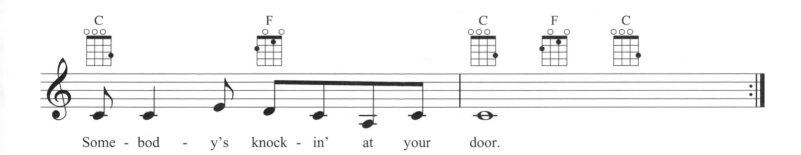

Some - bod - y's knock - in' at your door.

Sometimes I Feel Like a Motherless Child

African-American Spiritual

Standin' in the Need of Prayer

Traditional Spiritual

First note

𝄋 **Chorus**

Moderately

It's me, it's me, it's me, O Lord, ___ stand-in' in the need of

To Coda ⊕

prayer. It's me, it's me, it's me, O Lord, ___ stand-in' in the need of

Verse

prayer. 1. 'Taint my moth-er or my fa-ther, but it's me, O Lord, ___
2. 'Taint my dea-con or my lead-er, but it's me, O Lord, ___

stand-in' in the need of prayer. 'Taint my moth-er or my fa-ther, but it's
stand-in' in the need of prayer. 'Taint my dea-con or my lead-er, but it's

2nd time, D.S. al Coda ⊕ **Coda**

me, O Lord, ___ stand-in' in the need of prayer. It's
me, O Lord, ___ stand-in' in the need of prayer. It's

prayer.

Soon I Will Be Done
(Trouble of the World)
African-American Spiritual

First note

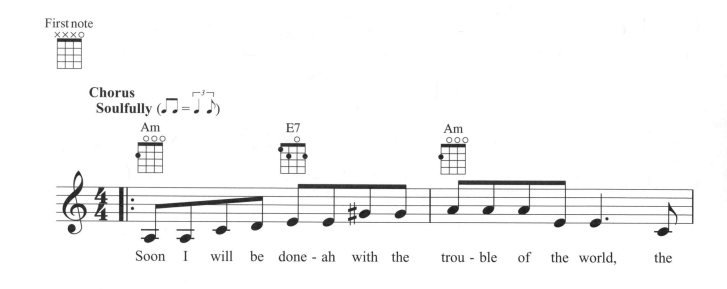

Chorus
Soulfully

Soon I will be done - ah with the trou - ble of the world, the

trou - ble of the world, ____ the trou - ble of ____ the world.

Soon I will be done - ah with the trou - ble of the world. Goin'

home to live with God.

Verse

1. No more   weep - in'   and   a - wail   -   in',
2. I   want _____ to   meet   my   moth   -   er,
3. I   want _____ to   meet   my   Je   -   sus,

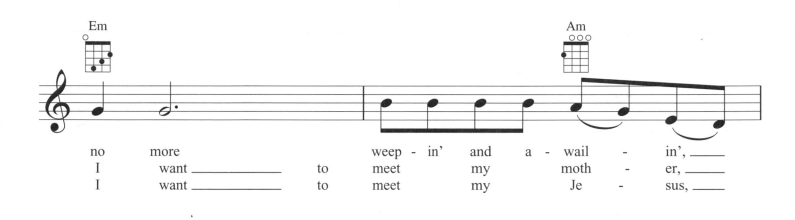

no   more   weep - in'   and   a - wail   -   in', _____
I   want _____ to   meet   my   moth   -   er, _____
I   want _____ to   meet   my   Je   -   sus, _____

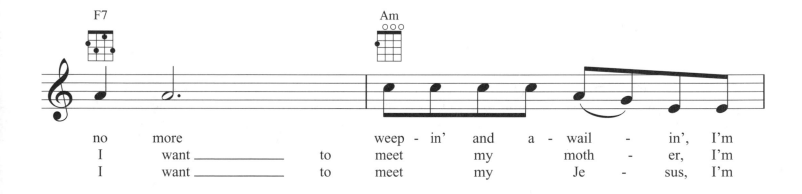

no   more   weep - in'   and   a - wail   -   in', I'm
I   want _____ to   meet   my   moth   -   er, I'm
I   want _____ to   meet   my   Je   -   sus, I'm

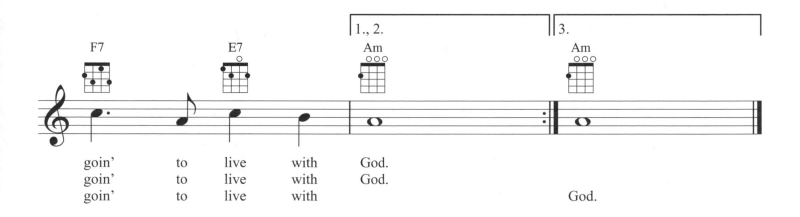

goin'   to   live   with   God.
goin'   to   live   with   God.
goin'   to   live   with   God.

Steal Away
(Steal Away to Jesus)
Traditional Spiritual

First note

Chorus
Moderately

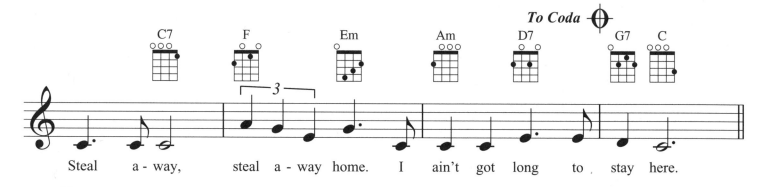

Steal a-way, steal a-way, steal a-way to Je-sus.

To Coda ⊕

Steal a-way, steal a-way home. I ain't got long to stay here.

Verse

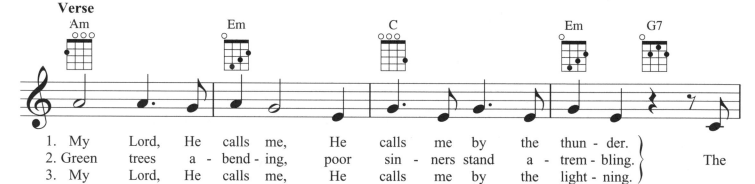

1. My Lord, He calls me, He calls me by the thun-der.
2. Green trees a-bend-ing, poor sin-ners stand a-trem-bling. } The
3. My Lord, He calls me, He calls me by the light-ning.

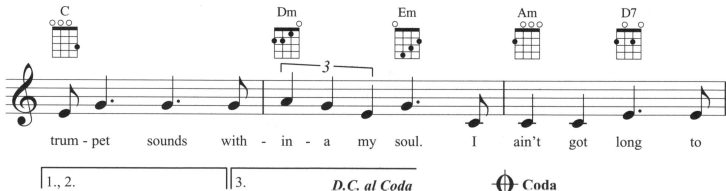

trum-pet sounds with-in-a my soul. I ain't got long to

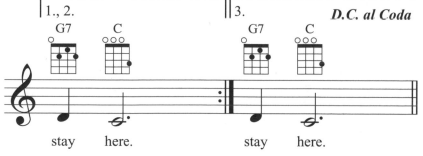

D.C. al Coda

1., 2.
stay here.

3.
stay here.

⊕ **Coda**

stay here.

Wade in the Water

Traditional Spiritual

Swing Low, Sweet Chariot

Traditional Spiritual

There Is a Balm in Gilead

African-American Spiritual

think my work's in vain, but
Je - sus is your friend, who,
can - not pray like Paul, you can

then the Ho - ly Spir - it re -
if you ask for knowl - edge, will
tell the love of Je - sus, and

1., 2.

vives my soul a - gain. _____
nev - er fail to lend. _____
say He died for all. _____

There __ is a

3.

D.S. al Coda

There _____ is a

Coda

soul.

This Little Light of Mine

African-American Spiritual

On Mon-day He gave me the gift of love, on

Tues-day peace came from a-bove, on Wednes-day told me to have more faith, on

Thurs-day gave me a lit-tle more grace. On Fri-day told me to

watch and pray, on Sat-ur-day told me just what to say, on

Sun-day gave me the pow-er di-vine, just to let my lit-tle light

D.C. al Coda

shine.

Coda

shine.

Were You There?

Traditional Spiritual

1. Were you there when they cru-ci-fied my Lord? _____ Were you
2.–4. *See additional lyrics*

there when they cru-ci-fied my Lord? _____ Oh! _____

Some-times it caus-es me to trem-ble, trem-ble, trem-ble. _____

_____ Were you there when they cru-ci-fied my Lord? _____

Additional Lyrics

2. Were you there when they nailed Him to the tree?
Were you there when they nailed Him to the tree? Oh!
Sometimes it causes me to tremble, tremble, tremble!
Were you there when they nailed Him to the tree?

3. Were you there when they laid Him in the tomb?
Were you there when they laid Him in the tomb? Oh!
Sometimes it causes me to tremble, tremble, tremble!
Were you there when they laid Him in the tomb?

4. Were you there when He rose up from the dead?
Were you there when He rose up from the dead? Oh!
Sometimes I feel like shouting glory, glory, glory!
Were you there when He rose up from the dead?